FUNDAMENTAL

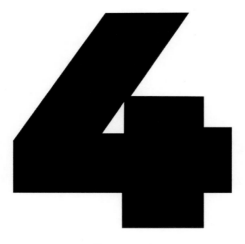

How you can elevate your mindset and boost performance in life

2020

Fundamental Four

How you can elevate your mindset and boost performance in life

Printed in the United States of America

First Printing, 2020

ISBN 978-0-578-64935-1

Hartley Capital Inc.

1100 Peachtree St. NE Suite 200

Atlanta, GA 30309

Third Edition

3 4 5 6 7 8 9

TABLE OF CONTENTS

7 ACKNOWLEDGMENTS

12 INTRODUCTION

FOCUS
Fundamental One

16 BLOCKING OUT THE NOISE
Chapter One

20 AVERAGE OF THE TOP FIVE
Chapter Two

26 END GOAL
Chapter Three

30 CONTENT IS LEVERAGE
Chapter Four

36 TELL YOUR STORY THROUGH BRANDING
Chapter Five

FINANCES
Fundamental Two

41 HAVE FUN WITH IT
Chapter Six

46 FIND, RESEARCH AND TRACK THE MONEY
Chapter Seven

49 ACCREDITED INVESTORS
Chapter Eight

54 POOLED INVESTMENTS PRIVATE FUNDS
Chapter Nine

59 FLATTEN YOUR EXPENSES AND
INCREASE YOUR INCOME
Chapter Ten

65 ASSETS > LIABILITIES
Chapter Eleven

FACULTY
Fundamental Three

72 PLAY YOUR ROLE
Chapter Twelve

76 DO BIG DEALS; THEN DO
EVEN BIGGER DEALS
Chapter Thirteen

83 EXECUTE! PROGRESSION
OVER PERFECTION
Chapter Fourteen

87 TEAM WORK
Chapter Fifteen

92 RUNNING A PRO-SYSTEM
Chapter Sixteen

97 ECO-SYSTEMS OVER PYRAMIDS
Chapter Seventeen

FAITH
Fundamental Four

102 BLIND FAITH: GOD IS IN COMPLETE CONTROL
Chapter Eighteen

105 ETHICS
Chapter Nineteen

109 GIVE IT ALL AWAY
Chapter Twenty

114 CONCLUSION

TABLE OF CONTENTS

ACKNOWLEDGMENTS

God, please increase yourself and decrease me. Thank you, God, for
granting me the serenity each and every day. Thank you for blessing
me with the opportunity to share this story.

Mom and Dad, thank you for always believing in me and supporting my dreams. Thank you for pouring into my life and investing in my future. Thank you for being the best listeners I could ever ask for. You have both always inspired me to dream big and to GO for it! I am so blessed to be your son! So, thank you for your unconditional love. I love you both so much.

Ashley, thank you for being with me while I pursued writing this book. Thank you for encouraging me when I was discouraged and helping me to never give up. Your support means so much to me.

Cheryl, thank you so much for all of your encouragement. Thank you for always supporting my visions and goals throughout the years

Dr. Minehart, thank you so much for your creative take on encouraging us to read in the 6th grade. You only gave us 20 minutes of reading for homework and nothing else. It sparked a love for reading in my life and inspired me to write even more. I will always remember that year in school. Also, I will always remember your amazing energy and kindness.

Shaunya and Kenneth Jr., aka JR, thank you for being an inspiration for me to become an entrepreneur. Both of you always found ways to build your own brands and businesses. You also always introduced me to new concepts and ideas.

Shaunya, thank you for always exposing me to new experiences, cultures, art, and events. You help me to see that the world is huge. JR, thank you for being such a great friend and a brother. Thank you for being here for me and for introducing real estate at an early age. Thank you to my niece and nephew, Amirah and Jeramiah. I love you both.

My Aunt Aimee, Aunt Dee, Great Aunt Gail, Aunt Ronnette, thank you for loving me so much. Each of you has played such a huge role in my life. I was able to travel overseas, have a car in high school, try new things, and make unforgettable memories because of you all. I love you always.

Thank you, Debbie Jones, for giving me my start during my summers back in Jersey.

My Uncle Gary, Uncle Eric, Great Uncle Richard, Uncle Wayne Bodden, and Uncle Alfred, thank you so much for your support and encouragement. Thank you for all of our laughs and the fun moments.

Uncle Eric, thank you for the unforgettable year that we shared when you moved back to Florida. I grew as a man when you moved back like never before. You pushed me to be better, and you always spoke so highly of me. I am proud of you, Uncle. Love you always.

To ALL of my cousins, thank you for being the best. I've had the pleasure of meeting new cousins in the last two years, and I am so thankful to do life together. We have the responsibility to carry our family's legacy and know we will do it well. I love you all, no matter how much distance separates any of us at any given time. We all are capable of doing incredible things.

Now, to all of my extended family of friends, thank you all for being in my corner. To Jabari, James, David, Darren, Stanley, Keishon, Garret, Chet, thank you for being the best friends I can have through College. I will never forget those memories.

Benny, Buddy, Dishon, Justin, Brandon, Beau, Stone, Aden, Mike, thank you for being my brothers growing up in Rockledge. Moving wasn't easy, coming from New Jersey, but the bright side is that my family grew.

My friends back in New Jersey Darron, aka DJ, Tony, Tramell, Shaun, Ibn, thank you for being the best friends ever, growing up in Jersey. It's been way too long since we last spoke. However, I still cherish the memories that we made when we were growing up.

I also want to acknowledge all of my amazing professors and teachers I've had over the years, thank you for pouring into me. Thank you, Michelle, for being a mentor and investing in SGA, the year I was under you. You will always have the best library ever. Thank you, Ms. Jacqueline, for taking the extra step to introduce me to SGA the year I was at Eastern Florida State College. Thank you, Professor Jones, for pushing me like never before academically and always believing in me.

Thank you, Professor Warford, for teaching two of the best classes I will ever take in my life. You are the true definition of a professor. Thank you, Professor Johnson for your genuineness and relatability. You're a leader with a vision, and I will always appreciate your passion for teaching and motivating.

To Ms. Taylor and to all of my amazing classmates in your classes. Those classes were life changing. We grew as a mini family that year, and I will always cherish that.

To Dr. Owens, thank you for being so understanding. You were seriously so inspiring to learn from. I am so grateful I was one of your students.

To all my pastors and youth church leaders, thank you for teaching me the word!

Lastly, to my grandparents, thank you for pouring into my parents and me. Thank you for taking the chances you did, to put out the family in a position to win. I love you always, and I pray I can contribute to continuing the legacy.

INTRODUCTION

If you're trying to figure out how to elevate your mindset and performance in life, then this book will serve as a kick start and a reference guide for you on your journey to success. It's time for you to focus on exactly what you want out of life, then go get it!

I'm Kerry Lee Hartley. I'm the CEO and Founder of Hartley Capital Inc., an investment firm. I've been a student of the game for as long as I can remember and simply fell in love with the journey.

I knew early on that life is what you make it. I made a conscious decision early on that I wanted to make the most out of life. I knew I wanted to serve others and win big with those around me. I knew I was born to be a leader.

As I grew older, it became impressively obvious that it's not enough to talk the talk, but you have to walk the walk. I learned that you have to make it happen through execution and consistency.

In this book, I want to share some of the lessons and principles I have learned in my pursuit of making the most out of life.

My wish is that you take all the information from this book to apply it to your journey to success. We all have a unique path we are walking on each and every day. My journey will differ from your journey, and that's OK because we can all learn from each other.

There are four parts to this book; Focus, Finance, Faculty, and Faith. Each of the four parts is what I have found necessary to make up the foundation for making the most out of life.

Focus is power, and there's no other way to phrase it. Once you are locked in on your target and have the right mindset, it's almost impossible to stop you. The only thing that can stop a focused person is themselves. I discuss how to build up your mindset, so you get out of your own way.

Getting your finances in order is key. Money is merely a resource. Once you are focused, you can tackle money and make it work for you. I breakdown some key points on how to put your money to work harder than it ever has before, to produce gains and profits.

The faculty discusses executing your vision. I speak on how we can tune into our purpose to spark our passion. I also discuss how to tap into your creativity.

Faith is the center of my life. I discuss the importance of keeping faith in my life. Even if you aren't religious, you still can find insight from this section that can help you along your journey to success. I also discuss how to keep the right perspective, even after finding success.

This book is not a textbook. I wrote this book to be the perfect conversation I was struggling to have with those around me. I'm very analytical and think very fast. So when I learn something that I find to be insightful, I want to share it with all those around me.

However, there's just never enough time to fit it all in one conversation. This book is my perfect conversation with you on how to make the most out of life.

FUNDAMENTAL
ONE

ONE

BLOCKING OUT THE NOISE

"If you chase two rabbits, both will escape"

Unknown

Focus is power. That may sound clichéd, but it's so true. When you can put your mind to something and stay determined not to stop until you reach the goal, that's power. You have to keep that focus, which takes an incredible amount of energy.

There are a few things to do to harness your power through focus. You must buy-in, plan for turbulence, and block out the noise.

Buying-in is essential for you to focus on the level you need to succeed. This is you committing to your vision and accepting nothing less. However, you have to decide to buy into your vision.

That being said, this also means that you have to buy into it knowing you may be the only one early on. That takes courage to do. So, don't let anyone tell you different because odds are, they don't see what you can.

On the other hand, you may face a ton of criticism and need to be able to withstand it. You can't give in to the popular opinion if you believe in what you're doing. So, buying-in will protect you from giving up on your goals.

Likewise, planning for turbulence is how you also prepare for the critics and stay focused. You have to put it in your mind that your journey is going to have obstacles, but that's OK, and you shouldn't run from it. Instead, embrace it and face it with the right mindset.

Most people don't plan for obstacles, and they believe it's always clear skies every day. Or even worse, they wait until they see no obstacles. So, that's unrealistic and will have you focused on the wrong things. Your vision has to be so big to you that it's worth pursuing it despite the obstacles that lie in front of you.

Blocking out the noise is a skill you can never stop improving. The noise is all around you, and it can seem to be never-ending. You face so many choices, options, opinions in this busy world. That's not changing — your resilience and all, in for your vision.

The noise around you can't affect you with the right mindset. It's about staying true to your journey and remaining locked in. That other stuff that isn't helping you progress, is only holding you back. Everyone will have an opinion to share with you about what they feel or what they think. Be very careful who you let in your ear because if you give them too much access, you may find that you take a detour from your route.

The key takeaway is that focus will be something you never stop working on in your life. You see the repetitive quote here that most things worth pursuing are an ongoing process. Trends come and go, but excellence lasts forever.

Don't take focus for granted, either. It's a great feat to have the ability to remain focused even in moments of chaos. No one can stop you when you lock into that level of commitment. Especially when your mission is pure and generous.

That focus will cut the noise around you and also attract the right energy you need around you. The negativity people may put out, won't last because the energy is weak and not focused.

Therefore, you should make what you're pursuing so big that it's slightly scary and still worth focusing 100 percent on. So, that's your why! Don't ever forget that 'why' because it fuels all that you do. It will evolve and grow as you evolve and grow. However, you need to remember that the principles and the foundation it was built on, won't change. Victory is yours for the taking, so stay locked in.

TWO

AVERAGE OF THE TOP FIVE

"You are the average of the top five people you spend the most time with"

Jim Rohn

We sometimes forget how much of our personality and habits come from those we spend time with. Have you ever stopped to wonder why you talk, act, and think the way you do? Also, have you ever picked up a personality trait from a family member or friend? Nine times out of ten you probably have, and that's completely normal.

We have a ton of learned behaviors we pick up from our close ones. The important thing is that we must be extremely conscious of the top five people we spend the most time with, whether they are friends, family, mentors, co-workers, or our spouse.

What's even more important is that we don't mistake spending time as only in person. In today's time, we can spend hours following other people's content via all the tools we have at our disposal. This is extremely valuable if you are intentional.

I like to say, even if you may not have family or friends going in the same direction as you, you can still intentionally spend time with like minds by soaking up their content. Read your ideal friend or mentor's book, watch their videos, or even listen to their podcasts or interviews. This is a way to leverage your tools to better your company.

There are four elements that you need to keep in mind when you're evaluating your top five people you spend the most time with in life. Likewise, each is important because it will help you stay intentional while choosing where you spend your priceless commodity of time.

The first thing is to watch how the person treats other people. This is especially important to watch for how they treat people who can't do anything for them. This is an ultimate test of their character. It can also be a window into how they may one day treat you or the people you care about in your life.

Sometimes, people put their best foot forward when you first meet, and it doesn't always allow you to see their full personality. However, when you get a chance to see that person interact with others, especially those who can add little to no monetary value to their life at the moment, pay very close attention.

This is especially true when following a person via their content or through social media. Now, of course, you can't judge a book by its cover, and there are legitimate attacks on people's charters and brands with slander. However, you have to use discernment and look past the surface as best as you can. Look into where they spend their time; look, and see if they have ever spoken on interactions with people. This may be a good place to start.

Another thing to watch is a person's habits. The internet has made it very easy for people to share their day to day life. It may not take long for you to learn what a person's habits are, whether you see them face to face every day or via the internet. So, you need to pay very close attention to any patterns or trends because this could be one of their habits.

A person's habits can show a lot about who they are. Some habits may promote self-discipline, and others may highlight a lack of discipline and potential addictions. Of course, everyone's journey is different, and it's best not to judge. You have to intentionally decide how you spend your time. If you are looking to build a habit that someone already has, spending time with them can better your chance at learning this habit.

For example, if you want to read more, then if you spend a fifth of your time with someone who is an avid reader, odds are you will become more of an avid reader. That works the same with not so healthy habits also, so be very careful.

Habits also give you insight into what a person may value in the current stage of their life. It can be a window into what they are focused on. It's also a great way to see if they are on their way to achieving their goals and vision. So, take a person's habits into account when it comes to where you spend your time.

The next thing we should watch for is someone's mentality. Perspective is everything because it's your mindset in action. People show you what their mentality is in their words. So, listen closely when people speak.

It's very important to watch someone's mindset when they face obstacles. Of course, when stress is present, we will have emotional reactions, but how long do they stay. If you notice a person facing challenges over the long haul with a positive perspective backed up by actions, it can be a great sign of a good mentality.

Another great thing is that if you are in a season when your mind isn't as strong as you would like it to be, who you spend your time with can affect your direction greatly. Getting around people with healthy mentalities will help you greatly. They will almost always hold you up when you feel like giving up. You will also pick up this mentality on your own.

The fourth thing you want to watch for is a person's beliefs. It's also very important to look at a person's self-belief. Confidence, NOT arrogance, is very important to have around you. You will be very surprised how those who you spend the most time with, affect your confidence.

A person doesn't have to share your every belief. Different beliefs are important to have in your circle, so you don't become insensitive or ignorant. One thing that is extremely important is that your core beliefs are shared with your top five. These are not your associates but your inner circle, so having a conflict constantly opposing your core beliefs open you up to go against your own core beliefs. Sometimes, this can be devastating. So be very intentional.

Please also consider this when you spend your time absorbing someone's content; also because that person's beliefs will be the undertone in all of their content. So, learn to read between the lines and listen carefully when someone shares their core beliefs.

The key takeaway is that you have to be careful and intentional about who you surround yourself with. Odds are, you will end up just like them. Keep company with those you are inspired to be more like.

Proverbs 27:17 "As iron sharpens iron, so a friend sharpens a friend." This captures the idea that when spending time with your inner circle, you are building each other up. So, don't take this lightly, especially when it comes to how you spend your time on the internet. It's not uncommon for us to spend more time on the internet than with people we know face to face. So be very intentional where you spend your time via the web and with whom.

THREE

END GOAL

"Without a game plan and without a strong sense of faith in what you're doing, it's going to be really hard to accomplish anything."

Nipsey Hussle

Your why has to be strong enough to drive your entire mission. It also has to attract the right team and inspire them to go for it. You have to get clear about number one, Your Why and number two, Your End Goal.

There are three things to keep in mind for your vision. You also need to keep these ideas in mind whenever an idea is sparked that you are going to pursue.

As I stated in my book Passion Purpose Creativity: How to Easily Gain Better Vision, "Vision to me is the ability to combine imagination and faith to create a map for greatness."

Imagination is an undervalued skill we have learned to forget as we grew older. As children, it seemed like all we did was use our imagination. We dreamed day and night and even acted out our dreams. However, as we got older, the majority of us stopped using our imagination and put that skill on the back burner.

However, we must not forget the power of imagination. This skill will help you gain a stronger perspective. Just like any other skill, you have to practice it often. This one is so worth practicing.

Here are three tips for gaining a stronger vision. The first is to use vision boards. The second is to keep it clear. The third is to manifest your vision. Moreover, each tip is incredibly helpful for creating a strong vision and an end goal.

For me, vision boards have been a strong tool I used to help me to get clear about my vision. It's a way to bring my thoughts to life, so I can see them daily. I like to post my vision board up on a wall, which I see very often so I can be reminded of my goals. It's also a great idea to use pictures if you can. But even without pictures, words can also help you. Also, the only rule for vision boarding is there are no rules. So be free and open to creating the perfect vision board for you.

Fuzzy targets don't get hit. When I first heard this, it was a very eye-opening moment for me. I feel my unique gift is my vision and ability to dream big. However, hearing this drove me to not only dream big but to plan just as big.

When you think about it, your chances of hitting a bullseye are higher, if your vision isn't blurred. The same thing goes for your visions and goals. You have to get super specific about what the end game looks like. This is because you will have to communicate this to a team that must buy into your idea and execute this with you.

Also, when times are tough, and you are facing trials and tribulations, a clear vision will help you keep perspective and motivate you to keep going.

The key takeaway here is that you can never lose sight of your WHY. You also have to have the vision clear enough for you and your team to see and refer to, when times are tough. Manifest your vision through positive speech, vision boarding, or in any way that works best for you.

FOUR

CONTENT IS LEVERAGE

"Attention is the most valuable asset."

Gary Vaynerchuk

The previous decade proved even more that attention is a huge commodity, which is traded every day. There are businesses being built and scaled on social media. The secret sauce is Content! Also, every one of us is capable of making it!

So, that's why you must find a way to push past any objections or limiting beliefs that you have about creating content. I'm almost sure that no matter how much you think you don't have relevant content to produce that truth be told, you do.

I am not advocating that you create vain material just to grow a following. On the contrary, I am suggesting that you speak your truth and discover your audience. We all have a voice, and sometimes we hide it, not knowing someone else can benefit from what we have to say.

The very first thing you must do to get started is to CREATE! It's not that complicated, no matter how much you want to make it complicated. Creating is an expression, and it is unique to your style. You have to practice it to find your voice, so don't worry about the end product when you are starting.

A lot of us freeze up when we finally try and tap into our creative side. This is because we have abandoned creativity for structure and routine. This is your time to break the monotony and spark innovation.

Now don't be fooled that your message may be as simple as you vlogging, or you writing blogs, or you creating art. Nevertheless, it's all art at its core if it comes from a unique place. Social media is just the platform that you can use to broadcast it.

So, what are you waiting for? Pick up the camera, open up word, or go to your creative place and CREATE. You deserve to produce, and no job or demand can take 100 percent of your time where you can't find time to do so.

When you get done producing your first project, then put it out into the world. Don't overthink it. If it feels right and it's coming from a pure positive space, then don't worry. If your energy is pure, the authenticity will be appreciated. Then move on and don't look back as that could potentially cause you to be self-critical. You don't need that, not now.

Once you get one under your belt and move on, you have a very important next step. Now you must CREATE EVEN MORE! Once you start this momentum, you don't want to lose it! It's going too well now for you to stop.

Don't you dare compare how many people viewed what you produce as a metric of success! That's a vanity metric at this point, as far as you are concerned. Double down on creativity and find joy in the process. Create for the pureness of the moment. Share what you can about life. Keep the energy positive, and you will have no worries.

If it comes from a place of pure intentions that don't harm or hinder others, then you have nothing to worry about. Even with all of that, people will still criticize and judge your decision to create. Take this advice in stride because they just haven't tapped into their creativity in a long time. Either that or they're jealous. This is the energy you can't afford to be around, or it will stifle your creativity.

Once you get the rhythm, then you can look at your work thus far. Don't do this if you haven't found pure joy in the process just yet. If you are still hung up on the end goal or perfection, then just keep creating. You will know when you're ready to look at your work with an open and positive mindset.

When that time comes, then you can build leverage. This is not a negative scheme; this is simply the truth. You have done what a lot of people don't want to or are too afraid to do. You created and launched your work into the world. Also, you stayed CONSISTENT! That is key.

Now at this time, you can evaluate your audience. With social media and other internet-based tools and platforms, this is easier than ever before. You want to discover who your core is, following the group. The number of people doesn't matter even if it's only one person. If you don't have an audience, that's OK; it simply means that you either haven't shared it enough, or you just have to create even more.

Once you narrow down who your core audience is, you can build a relationship with them. Discover more about what attracts them to your work. Get to understand who they are. This is your tribe. They can relate to your content and will be the biggest ambassadors in your next phase. You have successfully captured the attention of a niche audience.

From here, you can double down and focus more on the elements of your content that resonated with your tribe. Be careful not to water down your work and to remain relaxed as you were early on. Now is your time to create and challenge yourself to be free to create even more.

Congratulations, you have built an audience specific to your content organically. Over the years, people have been able to scale their tribe into incredible causes, businesses, and brands. So can you. The only thing to keep in mind is to stay consistent, have no ego in your art, don't sweat the vanity metrics or numbers, and stay pure, stay positive, and authentic. The rest will come.

The key takeaway here is to put in work and time. Putting out good but not always perfect content is essential. It builds the audience, captures people's attention, and grows your leverage. Once you have a seriously engaging audience, you now have an asset!

Award-winning artist Gucci Mane said in an interview, "The music is your assets man. You got 101 albums man you got a lot of leverage." He has successfully launched music and built a large catalog of content. It built him a following that carried into many other ventures.

I believe that music and albums can also be easily replaced by the content medium you use. It's not so much about the 'what' or the 'how' that matters, but instead, it is about your why. When you create from a place which is true to you, your audience will recognize it because it is relatable to them. So, again, the question is, what are you waiting for? Go out and create and then put it out into the world. Then repeat.

FIVE

TELL YOUR STORY
THROUGH BRANDING

"It takes 20 years to build a reputation and five minutes to ruin it. If you think about that, you'll do things differently."

Warren Buffet

We all have the opportunity to write our own story in life. This is part of our journey. Although everyone can criticize you or they can try and write your story for you. Why not get ahead of them and brand yourself?

The importance of storytelling cannot be understated. Today, we are blasted with more ads and more messages than ever before. Even our refrigerators have screens in them with WIFI connections. We see so many different sales pitches. Even billboards have to change screens with multiple ads running on them.

What we cannot do is allow our uniqueness to fade away. We all have something unique to share with the world, even if we don't see it at first. The skill we need now more than ever, is storytelling. Just because more messages are coming at us more than ever before, doesn't mean they're resonating more. At the end of the day, it all boils down to whether your story connects and relates to a demographic.

The other special thing to remember is being authentic in all that you do. A story doesn't even have to reach the masses. A very loyal group of early adapters plays a critical role as ambassadors to spread the message. The key is you gave your best to keep your message authentic and nothing less. The viewer is so alert to fakeness; they can sense it at a glance.

You may be thinking you can get it past the viewer, which may work for a little while. The problem is the moment the truth comes out; you devalue your story so bad, it may be nearly impossible to recover. Plus, viewers want to feel that they are a part of your story, so putting on a false persona could connect you to a group you don't speak for.

Your brand will also be a huge factor for your story. This goes for everyone, not just entrepreneurs, because we all have brands. Whether you know it or not, we all have brands attached to our names based on our consistent messaging. What we show the world on the day to day, becomes our unique brand which serves as a brand.

Often people attach themselves to brands for a variety of reasons. You begin to build an audience as you tell your story. If you are consistent enough, you may even have brand loyalty from your audience. That is very important because that's what causes someone to choose one brand over another.

Just think back to the time you may have seen someone choose a certain condiment brand over another. Or think back to a time where someone chooses a store over another. Now both options could have been very similar, almost identical outside of the brand. However, brand loyalty may cause a brand to be a clear answer to the recipient.

We also have to clarify one objection you may have toward this chapter. That is, you don't have a brand or an audience, and you don't need one. Please don't fall victim to thinking that brands are only for celebrities, businesses, products, etc. We all have some characteristics and uniqueness that represent us. You are writing your story every day, with each one of your decisions, actions, and habits. So why not be intentional writing your own story and telling it the way you know it should be told?

The key takeaway here is your story has a purpose no matter how insignificant you may perceive it to be. In a world with so many medians to connect and share your story, we're still in high demand for authentic stories that resonate with like minds.

There is no way around the importance of storytelling, authenticity, and branding. Globally, billions and billions of dollars are spent on advertising, marketing, and public relations. Your message also matters, no matter what you may think. We all have a story to share, and we all have at least one other person who can learn from our story.

Public relations (PR) is something that we should address in this chapter. Someone once told me PR is like a brand doctor. A publicist can either heal you from damage/illness, or they can help you prevent it from happening. Likewise, this applies to everyone because we all have our own brands. So even if you are a corporation or celebrity, take the time to be your brand doctor.

You may already use PR techniques and not even notice it. Keep your story authentic and protect your brand; you won't regret it.

Bill Gates, the founder of Microsoft, once said: "If I was down to the last dollar of my marketing budget, I'd spend it on PR!"

SIX

HAVE FUN WITH IT

Having fun with what you do, no matter how much you love it or else you run the risk of burning out. We can't afford to burn out because we have too many things to accomplish.

Your perspective is everything! If you can discipline yourself to have fun with it no matter what, you will build the right amount of resilience! Here are a few things to keep in mind to find out how you can have fun on your road to success.

Living with thanksgiving is the most fundamental way to find your joy. Gratitude helps you to keep focus and the right perspective. Start the day with gratitude, finish the day off with gratitude, and watch how your mood enhances. This is especially important when you lose motivation or face obstacles.

Gratitude is your secret weapon to defeat pride. You have no time to build an ego when you pursue gratitude. Gratitude gives you the right perspective. You can be sure that no matter how tough things look, there's at least one thing to be grateful for.

Don't allow your mind to put you in a valley where you can't see one thing to be grateful for. You can't fall for that trick that you have it worse than anyone else. Be very intentional about this and start small. It doesn't always need to be a huge list at first. Start by being grateful for at least one thing every day and remind yourself of it when you start and end your day.

Learning to laugh will also help you to have fun with your journey. This will be your remedy to any fear of other people's opinions. Learn how to laugh in life a little. You can't take everything so seriously, especially when learning.

Now I want to use an example, about the pressure that is used to create diamonds. However, pressure can be unhealthy, because you can't, and shouldn't live under constant pressure. Your ability to laugh at being flawed and loving yourself despite any flaws is a relief. Laughing will help you heal and love yourself even more.

Next, I want to clarify that what I am talking about is pure laughter, rather than laughter that's directed at someone. This is not laughter backed by judgment or criticism. Think of this laugh as pure as a baby's laugh. It's a laugh that shows you are happy to be alive. You are present at the moment, and you are OK with who you are. It's a confident laugh that heals you and those around you. Laughing is not a weakness; it's a strength. So, don't be so serious that you miss moments to laugh a little and to enjoy your time here.

Pushing past the desire to quit is done by falling in love with the process. Likewise, having a love for the process results from learning how to have fun with what you do. Everyone can learn how to do this, but it's a conscious decision we must make for ourselves.

The key takeaway here is that 9/10 times, the journey will fulfill you more than the end result. So, don't miss the moment by not finding the joy in the situation. We can find what we want to pursue. So, don't let someone else have control over you pursuing your dreams. Find the gratitude in all that you do and learn to laugh.

It's all about perspective. So, you should choose to have fun with it, regardless of how gray the moment can become. At the end of the day, that's life, we face ups and downs. However, we owe it to ourselves to enjoy life no matter how hectic things may look. A pure fun one that doesn't require any outside influence. A thrill off life itself.

FINANCES

FUNDAMENTAL
TWO

SEVEN

FIND, RESEARCH, AND
TRACK THE MONEY

"Show me the money!"

Jerry Maguire Movie

Deals get done worldwide every day. What is a deal, you may ask? If you ask me, it's simply just a transaction. Many deals happening each day can be traced back to the biggest companies. You have to know your competition even at the highest level. Creating a system in your operation to find, research, and track the money can put you in a step above others to stay in the know.

I would like to open your mind up to the practice following what the major players in your industry do to succeed. Also, if you are not running a business currently, that is totally OK; this can still apply to you.

One thing you also want to keep in mind is that most of the largest companies try to keep a sense of privacy with what they do. This not only allows them to be more mysterious but also allows them to keep their trade secrets confidential. Just take the idea of giving away all of your largest most profitable ideas to the public into account. This idea may allow your competition to take away your competitive advantage.

Luckily for us, we can find some information because the government requires most companies to give information on their general day-to-day operations. This is where we have to be, to discover what else we can locate to use to our advantage.

Again, if you are not in business, that is OK because this will still allow you to think larger and have a stronger perspective on how things really operate. Consider that you are looking to invest your hard-earned money for retirement and you're weighing all of your opportunities. There are a ton of options for your investment that managers will suggest you can invest in. However, if you are researching and following where the money is going at the highest level, also track and imitate what the leaders are doing in the economy.

In other words, you want to see the money, you want people to show you where the real money is going. Don't get left in the dust, wondering if what you are putting your money into is worth pursuing. Even if you are betting against or playing the devil's advocate, at least, you know what you are up against.

EIGHT

ACCREDITED INVESTORS

Accredited investor: "Being an Accredited investor under the federal securities laws, a company that offers or sells its securities must register the securities with the SEC or find an exemption from the registration requirements. The federal securities laws provide companies with several exemptions. For some of the exemptions, such as Rule 506 of Regulation D, a company may sell its securities to what are known as accredited investors. The term accredited investor is defined in Rule 501 of Regulation D."

Being an accredited investor is a great responsibility; it should not be taken lightly. Although that being said, you should also not be afraid to reach for accreditation status. An accredited investor has opportunities that everyday investors do not have the opportunity to invest. I'm a big fan of the book rich dad poor dad by Robert T. Kiyosaki. This book was a game-changer for me because it gave me my first introduction to accredited investors.

Accredited investors are a mystery because the SEC gives a very vague definition of what an incredible investor is. The verdicts of court cases are great opportunities to dismiss the vagueness of SEC's definitions. Again, I am not an accountant or a lawyer, so I cannot give legal or professional financial advice. But I can speak generally on this topic, which can open your eyes to something that you might not have known existed.

Reaching the accredited investor stage is all about intentionality. No matter if you were just beginning or you already have some good accessibility, you should still be intentional about reaching your goal. I knew early on, I wanted to be an accredited investor because I was very interested in start-ups and new and exciting ideas. Sometimes, you will not be the main catalyst for launching these new business models or new ideas. However, you can invest in start-up ideas early on with the credit in its investor status. Sometimes, for outside investors, capital can be a lifeline for start-ups in new ideas coming to life.

The current accredited investor requirements can be found on the SEC website. I like to look at the requirements for individuals to become accredited. However, please remember that between the time I wrote this book, you would be reading the rules that could have changed.

The two requirements I look at are based on your annual income or your net worth. This gives me a great visual for a goal to reach, as I am making a financial decision on a day to day.

Once you know what it takes to be an accredited investor, it can also help you to discover who is really accredited and who is not. Although being an accredited investor is not a guarantee that you will succeed. However, it does at least show you that you are in a position to withstand against the risk the everyday investor cannot.

Part of finding, researching, and tracking the money will require you to look at other accredited investors. When networking, you may also want to see if the people you are talking to are also accredited as well. This is because accredited investors can invest in riskier, more private opportunities that everyday investors cannot.

Even if you are not in a position to invest in the same vehicles as accredited investors, it is never too early to start learning how you might want to operate, to become an accredited investor. A big part of this is also getting past the smoke screens and seeing if people you meet can back up their talk by walking the walk.

As an accredited investor, you can also get into a position in which they are learning by working with their advisory team. Your accountants, lawyers, bankers, and other advisors can be the difference in you growing your wealth or losing your wealth. Likewise, due diligence and risk of valuation are some of the most important things you can do before investing in anything. You have to trust your instincts as well, and you should surround yourself with the right advisory to make the best decision you can. Now, although you never can be perfect, you always want to strive to make the best decision no matter the circumstances.

If you are not currently accredited, networking with accredited investors is your best bet. You cannot expect someone in that position to entertain one-sided relationships. In everything you do, you want to be looking for ways to add value. This is no different because accredited investors are looking for genuine relationships that also bring value.

It is also very important to make sure the person you were studying has great financial literacy. Money can be earned from active income, which does not necessarily mean the person is very smart with investing. Knowing how to earn money differs from knowing how to invest some money. So, please do not misunderstand this point because earned income is treated differently in the Techsystems, than most passive income is treated, generally speaking.

Can you think about where accredited investors might learn from? Can you think about where accredited investors spend their time? Can you also think about what accredited investors might value the most? It isn't too far-fetched to find an accredited investor to mentor you as well.

This journey is a marathon, not a sprint. However, there are times during the marathon when you may need to accelerate. I challenge you to see how soon you can get to accredited investor status. Why not? What do you have to lose? This gives you the use to get to accreditation that will only be magnified at the next phase. Go after it hard, and don't back down! People will try to doubt your ability to get there or even discourage you from trying things they don't feel comfortable doing. It would be so easy if everybody would be an accredited investor. But remember the journey is also a mental game where you have to outsmart sometimes even yourself. You have to go against what feels comfortable to do, what is actually wiser and more beneficial in the long run.

Think about being accredited early in your life and having access to some of the most ground-breaking companies and investment opportunities before everyone else. This could be a game-changer for you and your family.

Whether or not you can still want to have a good understanding of what it means to be accredited, this will help you have the right perspective whenever you are thinking about your financial moves. The goal is not to just be accredited but is to be very wise in your investments. This will allow you to continuously progress and to make better decisions as you gain more experience.

NINE

POOLED INVESTMENTS
PRIVATE FUNDS

"Private funds are pooled investment vehicles that are excluded from the definition of an investment company under the Investment Company Act of 1940 by section 3(c)(1) or 3(c)(7) of that Act. The term private fund generally includes funds commonly known as hedge funds and private equity funds." -

www.Sec.gov

Full disclosure, I am not a lawyer, an accountant, or a licensed financial advisor. I cannot give you legal or financial advice. Please seek professional counsel to seek answers for any questions or concerns. I am merely giving general information. Also, depending on the time you read this book, the regulations could or might not change.

Historically, Private funds and other private pooled investments have allowed accredited investors to invest in alternative investments. Once you reach accredited investor status, you can too.

However, you may feel encouraged to launch your own fund. That is also very possible, as well. Whatever your choice is, I want you to be as educated on the subject because a great deal of business gets done through funds.

Investopedia.com defines pooled funds as a "portfolio of money from many individual investors that are aggregated for the purposes of investment."

Investopedia.com also mentions, "With pooled funds, groups of investors can take advantage of opportunities typically available to only large investors."

This is vital that you reread the last sentence, "typically available to only large investors." This is very vague when you think about it. What qualifies an investor as large?

Large typically means institutional investors. Investopedia.com also says that there are 6 types of institutional investors generally "endowment funds, commercial banks, mutual funds, hedge funds, pension funds and insurance companies." As you can see, large is actually very large!

This is why pooled funds are so incredible. They open up the door for other investors to invest in some of the biggest and best deals out there. However, the risk also increases, but pools help spread the risk across all investors.

Being accredited opens up the door to be placed right in the mix of many of these deals. You will have the legal access to invest in many of these funds based on the current SEC rules. Although, that being said, you still have to position yourself to invest in the fund that best fits your portfolio needs. Each fund has its own function and own strategy. Work with the fund that makes the most sense for your goals.

"Most alternative investment assets are held by institutional investors or accredited, high-net-worth individuals because of their complex nature, lack of regulation, and degree of risk," says Investopedia.

The key is to remember that these investments are alternatives from your conventional investments. However, they may not take a big chunk of your portfolio. Generally, they are at high risk, but with high rewards. On the other hand, you still have to do your due diligence and seek professional counsel. Make sure it's right for you and your goals.

A new pooled fund again can be created. A few general tips can point you in the right direction. Seek an attorney and build a team, stay connected, and research, research, research!

I cannot stress enough the importance of building a team with professional legal and accounting counsel. There are laws and regulations, which you MUST follow to stay out of legal trouble. Also, you will be handling other people's money. Likewise, that alone is a huge responsibility and shouldn't be taken lightly!

You also want to stay connected to the markets and your investors. Depending on the type of fund you launch and the regulations, you may have to raise money in a certain manner. Nevertheless, you will probably have to raise money, and this takes planning. So, it's best to be in the right rooms with the right people well before you raise capital.

You also want to research like you've never researched before. If you can study the moves that other funds have made. Go to the

SEC site and read it front to back and get very familiar with your competition. Some funds are very secretive in nature, so you may have to dive really deep. Also, ask your attorney, especially if you hire one who is very familiar with securities. They can be a great source of information you can tap into.

The key takeaway is to learn about pool investments and pooled funds. At some point, you want to max out your traditional investment opportunities and may want to invest in alternative investments. However, you may also find that you might even want to launch your own fund.

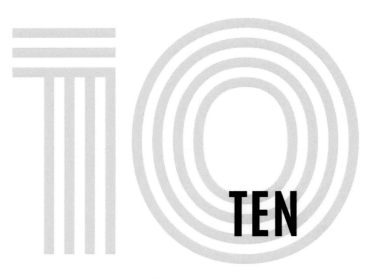

TEN

FLATTEN YOUR EXPENSES & INCREASE YOUR INCOME

Your income is a huge contributor to your wealth-building. Your expenses can be one of the biggest thieves to your wealth-building.

Income is something that has taught me the toughest lesson early on as an entrepreneur. I mean the absolute toughest. Taking an idea from paper to action is not always the easiest feat! Coming from the idea that the only way to make income is to trade my time for money (a job) to turning ideas and business models into cash is a challenge.

The truth of the matter is that no matter what way you make an income, you have to leverage it and take full control over it.

Besides taking full control over your income, you have to also take control of all your expenses. There are so many small things that steal your income from you with each and every paycheck. There is a ton of highly sophisticated campaigns and strategies that companies use to take the pain out of spending money. Trust me, you have to be wiser and very intentional with any expense you have. There is very little sympathy for you once you sign up to take on a ton of expenses. Sometimes, once you get into the commitment, it can be very hard to maintain it and/or get out of it.

On your road to becoming an accredited investor and beyond that, you have to flatten your expenses, so as your income increases, your expenses don't steal your income. This mindset will change your financial behavior and cause you to look at income completely differently.

Here are a few techniques for you to implement to maximize your income, control your expenses, and protect your financial health.

First, you must keep an income and keep an emergency savings fund. This is non-negotiable. You have to keep money coming in if you need savings. This will keep you at ease mentally and allow you to make a clear decision.

Especially as an entrepreneur, your number one goal is to save up savings with six months' worth to cover all your expenses. It can be the most discouraging thing to hear this at first because your passion and vision are so strong for your business idea.

The key is if you can get this handled in the beginning, you avoid having a larger financial roadblock later. You run the risk of having to stop growing your business to get your finances back in order if you don't. The last thing you want to do is lose momentum because it is extremely hard to gain that back if you lose it.

The next technique is to know your minimum living expenses to reach your goal. Then to live at or below this number. This will help you to keep a higher percentage of your income to invest. Take this very seriously! It may seem extreme, but this is how you stay thriving. If every time your income increases, you raise your expenses, then you haven't made much progress.

So, keeping a positive margin between your income and your expenses, will give you more power with your money. The idea is to not get caught up with how much you make but rather how much you keep after expenses. If you make a million dollars and spend a million dollars on all liabilities, you made nothing. That's looking wealthy vs. being wealthy.

This isn't meant to keep you being extreme and spending nothing. Instead, this is to allow more of your income and money to be invested and to work harder than you ever can. I will never forget being introduced to the perspective that some people have so little expenses that they can invest as much as up to 50 percent of their income and sometimes even more. That's freedom to me; not having to live above my means early to invest like no one else early on. The fruits that come from that, could produce enough passive income, so that the life that was once above my means is now well within my limits.

On top of managing income and expenses, you also need to know your end goal number. What does "retirement" look like to you? I put quotations there because retirement doesn't always have to be age, but instead, it is more so a number.

You need to determine what your nest egg needs to look like and what lifestyle you want to live in "retirement." Of course, you have to take into account that there's more to investing than traditional retirement accounts. Besides, there are also some, which provide dividends sooner and don't have an age requirement.

I'm not here to argue what's better than the other. You can do both! But I am here saying that you MUST know your numbers. There are three numbers I say you should know with no hesitation. If you know your survival number and you are doing well in terms of numbers, then you'll be a wealthy number.

Your survival number is what you need after you cut ties with having a job that you have enough to cover all expenses and get by without having to pick up another job.

This isn't the most ideal number to live for, but it's your base number. Anything below it, and you won't fair well without keeping a job. This I argue, is what a large amount of us are betting on for retirement. We just "hope" we can make enough to keep the lights on and not have to get back in the workforce.

Also, this number is frequently attached to an age that is above 60 years or older. That is no way to live. You still have to know this number to keep perspective. Anything below it, and you're in deep trouble.

The next number that you need to know is your well-off number. Your well-off number is the one that allows you to breathe. You can treat yourself and your family to a few things a year and not be in any danger.

There is more freedom at this number because you can do more with your money. Again, this number can be reached with other investments outside of traditional retirement accounts. The key is to remember the earlier you start living off your money and no job, the more of it you need. That's ok because when you reach this point, you probably already know earned income wasn't solely the answer to financial freedom.

Your well-off number also allows you to make a choice. You will have to choose if this is enough or should you pursue the next level. Odds are you are under too much stress at your survival number to think as clearly. At your well-off number, you have some room to breathe, and you just might say this is enough.

The third number that you want to know without hesitation is your wealthy number. For all you dreamers out there, this may be your favorite number. This is the number that allows you to do things that you may have only dreamed of. You can give and do more than you ever thought you could.

This number may not be to everyone's taste, but I still urge you to know it. It's important because it will allow you to have a quantifiable number that you know is your wealthy number. That way, you have a gauge to let you know where you stand. This number may also serve as your motivation when you are just getting started. Knowing this number will help you keep perspective on where you're headed.

Your key takeaway here is to be determined about flat lining your expenses. Do this even while you are at a place where you aren't starving because discipline will take you further. This will allow you to invest more in your income, no matter what you make into retirement and assets.

Again, your income is a huge contributor to your wealth-building. Your expenses can be one of your biggest thieves to your wealth-building.

So, you need to be intentional regarding where the money you bring in is going!

ELEVEN

ASSETS > LIABILITIES

Assets appreciate over time, and liabilities depreciate over time, generally speaking. As Robert T. Kiyosaki also illustrates, "an asset is something that puts money in your pocket, and a liability is something that takes money out of your pocket."

This is a very key thing you want to grasp early on, and not forget. You will start to move differently once you take this into account and act on it. You will see things through a different lens. You will most certainly handle money much differently.

This can be a very hard lesson in the beginning, especially if you have been taught something completely different. The lessons you learn from your family and friends can determine your current beliefs. The good thing is if you aren't happy with your current beliefs, you can work now to change them. Here are a few tips for you to increase your assets and take control of your liabilities.

You must decide to first remove all guilt you have if you don't own even a single asset but own many liabilities. Remember, you are running your race. So, things can change, and your past doesn't have to be your future no matter how bleak it may seem.

Next, you must also make the decision to remove pride if you own a ton of assets and fewer liabilities. Just because you're in a better situation financially than others doesn't open the door for you to have a huge ego. This can close doors for you. It's OK to be grateful for success, but pride and ego typically will only work against you in the long run.

Both of these battles are faults in your mentality. So, you have to be very conscious of what you are feeding your mind on a day to day. This is about financial literacy, so don't let the emotional battle deter you from success.

Once you find out what an asset is, you may look at your possessions and spending habits and feel very vulnerable. So, please DON'T worry because it's OK to feel this emotion when you're starting out. However, please keep in mind that you cannot allow this doubt to go any further. Your situation can change, and it will change! So, remove your guilt and replace it with faith and determination.

You seriously want to learn this lesson early! It doesn't matter what age you are when you learn that not all things are assets that put money in your pocket, then you have to take the intentional asset. Now full disclosure; there are a ton of materials that are liabilities and are fun. However, it's about being financially literate and knowing that your assets are at least triple your liabilities. You want to be wealthy, not look wealthy.

You should also be careful that you don't base your success on the wrong metrics. You basing your success on luxury items is a never-ending battle. There is always a new and shinier item that will come next. To make things even more complicated, the next big thing may just be a relaunch of a retro item. So please be mindful not to fight the wrong battle. As you will probably know, things can be fun to own and experience. However, if you have expensive tastes without enough assets, then it will be recipe for disaster!

This is how I fell in love with real estate. It was my door to buying assets. It was one of the easiest concepts of assets vs. liabilities to grasp. If you think about a house, it can be an asset or a liability depending on its function. Living in a house with a mortgage and other expenses will only take money out of my pockets. However, if I own a rental property that throws off a net profit after all expenses are paid, it's an asset. Keeping that property rented out and in good condition is in my best interest. It's also in my best interest to reinvest some of my earnings into gaining another rental property to grow my assets.

It's all about perspective. Stop and think for a second how the manufacturer of the item views the product you are buying. They are on the other side of the transaction. Are they a business owner whose business is an asset but sells you a liability? Think about it, their business puts money in their pocket, but your purchase may only be taking money out of your pocket.

Sometimes it is a sell or be sold the world. Again, there is nothing wrong with having an expensive taste if it's prioritized correctly. Also, the type of income you are spending matters when buying these shiny objects. Spending all of your earned income can be very costly when it's not being spent into enough assets.

You also want the asset you invest in to ultimately turn into passive income. Earned income means you have to be there to make an income. Passive income means you don't have to be there to make an income. That means your income doesn't have to depend on you being there! So, this can change your LIFE!

The key takeaway is that you have to be very careful with what you call an asset. You can't allow liability to be mistaken for an asset. You will lose out big time!

This simple mistake can have you building a false reality that you have a bunch of assets that are just draining your pockets. Think about maintenance and upkeep. Also, look at the item's current value vs. the price you paid for it. This will also help you to negotiate better when you do buy things. The price you pay doesn't always show you the full story. It's OK to negotiate because when the final sale is made, you will be left with the bill.

You will know an asset when you see one. Soon, you will also learn how to determine which assets are better than others. At some point, you will see that some assets are more profitable than others. This is what wealthy people do. They let their money work hard for them. They get to a point where they stop working hard by trading time for money but instead invest money for it to work 100x harder to make more. You will never outwork money! It never sleeps, it doesn't need to eat, and it does whatever you invest it to do. So, the goal is to manage it wisely.

Invest in an asset over liabilities! Especially ones that create passive income. Once you have enough passive income coming in with excess, you can then afford those liabilities because let's be honest, they can be pretty fun.

Also, what you feel like is fun, may not be to buy shiny items and to live lavishly. You may have other ideas on how to spend money. Like being extremely generous or supporting a cause or research efforts. The key is being able to do this without stress because you are financially free.

Just because something isn't throwing off a monetary profit, it doesn't mean it doesn't have other benefits. There are tons of ways you can share your resources, which helps so many people. The game-changer is being able to do that lavishly and still living a very comfortable life. You don't have to choose. You very much can have both. It's very important and rewarding for you to be generous with wealth without compromising on living a comfortable life.

FUNDAMENTAL
THREE

TWELVE

PLAY YOUR ROLE

Someone has to be the tip of the umbrella, and someone has to be the rib of an umbrella. No role is more important than the other because they both need each other to execute the function of the umbrella.

You have to keep your eyes open for opportunities to connect the right people. That's a skill in itself to be able to see that seemingly unrelated people can be a key part of each other's mission.

We all serve as a leader in some shape or form even if it's a situational leadership role. It doesn't particularly matter how large the operation that you lead is. You are still a leader. This comes with responsibilities that must be taken into account.

Leaders are seen as the tip of the umbrella. However, just having a tip isn't much of an umbrella. True leaders know how to scout and recruit the right team and to allow them to shine to execute the function of the whole.

Mastering three skills will be a never-ending journey of yours as a leader. You will constantly be scouting/recruiting talent, connecting people, and playing your position.

Being a scout and a recruiter is going to be so essential. You will have some turnover in your circle, just like any other organization. People come and go, then they even return. It usually shouldn't be taken personally but seen as a season in your life. The key is to always keep an eye out for talent. We all can do this contrary to popular belief. The main thing you have to do is to keep your eyes and ears open. You never know when and where you might come across the right people.

You also have to play offense and defense when it comes to recruiting. Sometimes, you have to actively reach out and win over talented people. Don't overthink it. This can be as simple as a thank you card after a great conversation. The next thing is you also have to play some defense to keep talent. This is done by listening to people and learning their needs and wants. You also have to add value in the relationship, and this is not a one-time thing. Also, keep in mind that people you meet now and see talent in may take years to have a common goal position you both can connect with. But that's where defense comes into play; you must defend against being forgotten and making them feel forgotten. Stay in touch. It costs nothing to check up on someone.

Connecting the people is the next part of this equation. This is why you were scouting and recruiting in the first place. This is where you add your true value. It's about being able to connect people to cause something they couldn't do alone, even if it brings you nothing in return. People gravitate towards people who know the right people.

Having this vision will take time to develop. However, what you probably don't realize is that you do this already. It can be something as small as picking the right friends to accompany you to the right events, which shows that you have the skills. You wouldn't invite your friends that despise sports to head out to the local sports grill to watch the game.

Now in this get-together, you may invite one co-worker friend and one childhood friend who both like sports. However, you also know that both have a similar goal to mentor the local youth through coaching sports. Due to you connecting the two, they were able to start the conversation that day to launch a non-profit for this cause. This is the power of connecting people because you take into account something bigger than yourself; you can connect the right people at the right time.

You must always play your role no matter how large or small. This is vital for the team. Sometimes, your role may call for you to step up for someone else, or maybe it's to lead the ship. Regardless, you don't want to leave your team high and dry.

Playing your role requires you to be egoless and selfless. The team and the bigger picture must be built around why. People can sense this too from miles away, so don't try to fake it.

Get very clear on what position is also performed at your best ability. You shouldn't take it easy because your role at the surface level doesn't seem very significant. News flash, every position is significant; the key to being invaluable is in your work ethic. Hustle hard even if no one is watching. That's having integrity in your work, and that's sometimes hard to come across.

Another part of playing your role is to keep a record of what you do. If you aren't able to show up, that means someone has to step up and fill in. It's part of your responsibility to make it as easy and seamless for the person to execute in your role. If it's extremely specific to your skillset, then it's understandable that it won't get done perfectly. For most situations, that's OK, you don't need per-fection; instead, you need progression. If, for some reason you do need perfection and need a clone, then preparation well before this situation should call for you to pour into a protege to be ready to step in, without missing a beat.

The key takeaway here is No one is bigger than the team. Each responsibility is important! So please stop downplaying or overvaluing your role if you are. No one is self-made at its core. Maybe early on, you can get by with very minimal help, but that's not sustainable.

Be the team member you always dreamed of. Also, build the team you have always wanted if you don't have one. You may even need to join a team. Regardless of how, just remember, you're always scouting or recruiting. Remember to also connect people constantly; that skill is invaluable. Also, play YOUR position to your very best ability every day! Have a work ethic like no other, even if no one else is watching. That is the true test of your character as a leader to know that you don't have to be watched to do right.

An invaluable leadership trait is the ability to connect people with people and to build a team. You will find yourself being a linchpin to many teams by being able to accomplish this.

You may have to be the tip of the umbrella at times, and other times you may need to be the rib. Everyone on the team should be working together to build the team, not just the tip of the organization.

Seek opportunities to scout and recruit new pieces to your team or even just great contacts to have. I choose to never miss an opportunity to collect someone's phone number or email, who has a specific skill or trait. I do this even if, at the moment, I am not actively going to connect with them right away.

Be the connector for people in your circle. That skill can be priceless the more and more you practice. Being the person that can see how connecting two or more people at the right time will make you a stronger leader. So, remember, you don't only have to recruit for your immediate team, but you can also network on behalf of others in your network.

I can speak on the idea of playing your position because I have done the opposite and saw the consequences. When you are active in your role, please play your role. It may not be the most ideal position, but as long as you're on that team, play your position. You start to hinder the team when you get in the way of others. Now the one exception is stepping up for others when you're down a team member. Other than that, play your position.

THIRTEEN

DO BIG DEALS; THEN DO
EVEN BIGGER DEALS

More times than not, it takes more energy to do the bigger deals than it does the smaller ones. However, the outcome is much larger. Now when we say deals, I am really talking about transactions involving the purchase or acquisition of an asset. Also, a move you made to level up professionally. But bigger can mean something else for you and your journey in life.

The idea that smaller is easier and safer isn't always true. The bigger deals may take a stronger team, but you CAN still get them done. Just, in the beginning, you have to give more to get more.

When doing bigger deals, you must first start by doing research. This is also referred to as due diligence. The bigger the deal, the more you want to double and triple check your due diligence. This is because you want to minimize your risk and exposure.

Odds are you won't be able to eliminate the risk altogether, but that's OK. In fact, if there were absolutely no risks, odds are the upside would also be very little or non-existent. Risk isn't your biggest problem, lack of research, and proper due diligence is.

Professionals know that to last at the highest level, you must calculate what it takes. Luke 14:28 NLT says, "But don't begin until you count the cost. For who would begin construction of a building without first calculating the cost to see if there is enough money to finish it?"

The same applies to you in everything. Now, of course, regardless of the size of the venture, you still have to do your research. Please just know that as the deal increases, the level of research will also increase.

Now don't get discouraged if the deal requires a deep level of expertise to execute the due diligence. That's where having the right personnel comes into play. You don't have to be the smartest person in the room. In fact, you really don't want to be the smartest person in the room. Tackling larger deals will almost force you to build the right team. If not, you will probably lose out big time or not even have a chance at bidding for it.

Your personnel will be your lifeline for tackling such a large feat. It also requires you to lose your ego. Play your role, and don't worry about not doing everything. That's OK, and you shouldn't feel bad. Also, don't allow others to write you out of the deal.

Give more to get more. It will come back to you. If you bring value no matter how large or how small, you should be compensated for it. Of course, you need to remember that this is not the time to be greedy either.

Sometimes, people see the large or shiny reward on the other side of the deal and want to try and keep it all for themselves. You have to remember that there will be other deals. So, make sure your team wins too.

This is called having an abundance mindset and not having a scarcity mindset. So, it's a belief in a world that is full of abundance, where there's enough for everyone to win. To attract the personnel, you probably need to accomplish things at the highest level; it's a prerequisite that your mindset is right.

This is important to remember everywhere in your life. Give more to get more but don't get caught up on the "get more" part. This will always come, but only if you never stop focusing on the give more part. Give more value; always, that's the key and watch it all come back your way. Then give even more back. Also, you need to remember that you do not need to over complicate it.

The key takeaway here is to go for the big ones too. It doesn't always take decades to get into bigger deals. You can leverage your relationships to build strong enough teams to tackle more complex deals, but just remember you can't be greedy! Your value is your vision and bringing the pieces together.

In real estate, I never know when I might come across the deal of a lifetime. It may be a deal that seems way out of my league and something I should pass on. However, I won't pass on it without first weighing my options. No deal is off the table without first doing my due diligence. If I like it and want to pursue it, then I dive deep into researching all aspects.

After a preliminary look, I calculate the cost and determine what personnel I will need to accomplish the deal. That's why I also won't pass on the deal because I know the best talent will want it to be worth their time.

So, with a good enough deal on my table, I use it to attract the best talent I can. Basically, I feel my team with smarter people than myself. From there, I get out of my own way and let go of my ego and find ways to add value to the team.

Sometimes, that means just piecing together the team, and other times it requires more of my skills. However, in all opportunities, I seek to give more value in all areas I can. When it's all said and done, you will either have accomplished and completed the deal, or you have gained even more experience.

Regardless of the outcome, you come out ahead. You can't lose if you lose the ego because it will always teach you a lesson.

Sometimes, Bigger is better and bigger isn't always more work. Don't be so quick to write yourself out of the deal. Be bold but back it up with due diligence, building the best team, and losing your ego and adding value.

FOURTEEN

EXECUTE! PROGRESSION OVER PERFECTION

"Vision without execution is hallucination."

Thomas Edison

I'd rather have progression over perfection. The pursuit of progression is OK but not attempting or giving up because you lack perfection, is not acceptable.

The one true way to have progression is by executing your vision one step at a time. You will find a ton of lessons on your journey. So, I guess that is the reason people, as I say, "fall in love" with the journey or the process. But you will hinder your growth if you never execute on your goals and manifest despite perfection.

Seth Goodin once mentioned in his book Linchpin the idea of planning to ship, in spite of perfection. This idea was a game-changer for me because it relieved a ton of pressure off my shoulders. It gave me the OK to be almost perfect in what I do. The bigger and more important picture is that you manifested your idea and work.

Don't fall victim to the idea that this means we can produce any type of work. This means we should still strive for perfection but be OK with putting it out into the world even if it's not perfection. We have to get out bright ideas and art out of our heads and into the world. We are all artists in our way, and we all want what we produce to be flawless. The reality is that the world doesn't need perfection because that will never come. Remember to ship your work in spite of perfection and accept the productive criticism in stride.

Success is a journey, and progress is our fuel. Falling in love with the journey is so key to your happiness. We want to fall in love with the end goal but fail to realize that the journey is where we find our true happiness. That is where you gain so much knowledge, endurance, and memories.

Now, please don't get me wrong; we want to accomplish our goals. However, our, your, basically all and any type of success is always a moving target. Only finding happiness in reaching your goal will be an exhausting battle. You have to find peace in the process.

That's why progression is so key. Realizing that each step in the right direction, no matter how large or small it is, is still progress. That it is the motivation there that will carry your momentum.

You must only be concerned with putting your best foot forward, given the tools you have at your disposal at the time. It's OK that you may not have all the tools you wish you had or all of the help you may have needed.

What matters is you finish what you started! That's commendable, to say the least. Everyone doesn't always finish what they start, so please don't take that lightly. Run your race. Mind your own business. Whatever you want to call it, it doesn't matter, but please remember that you are only concerned with being the best you can. So, don't fall victim to comparing yourself to others.

The key takeaway here is to remember not to create paralysis by analysis. Get it out of your head and bring it to life. Just make sure it comes from a place of honesty and genuineness. The rest will work itself out over time.

You will never know the full potential for your ideas until you bring them to life and put them to the test. That is what pushes progress forward. Again, success is a journey, and progress is our fuel. Falling in love with the journey is so key to your happiness.

FIFTEEN

TEAM WORK

"Talent wins games, but teamwork and intelligence win championships."

Michael Jordan

You never stop growing as a team! But no matter what business or industry you're in, you must have a team. You can't take this lightly because true success and fulfillment don't come from solo endeavors. No matter what someone says at face value, there is always someone else who contributed to their success.

Building a team takes effort, and it is an ongoing journey. There are a few tips and techniques that can help you on your journey to building a team.

The first technique I suggest for you is to ensure that the people you bring on your team fit the T.H.E.Y. characteristics. T.H.E.Y. stands for tough, honest, energetic, and yes. I was introduced to this concept at my church during leadership training.

Having tough team members in this context means they are tough in the right areas. You should see toughness in the emotions and mentality first and foremost. Depending on your goals and aspirations, you also should see toughness spiritually and physically.

You want to make sure your team members are also honest, totally and brutally. You want to make sure that there is transparency with the team and also that they are honest amongst themselves. Teams really can't move forward when there are secrets that hinder progression.

It's vital that you also check your team's energy level. A team member should ideally have a positive energy that always brings excitement. They should also bring a sense of relief when they are around, helping to bear some of the load on the team. Also, they must have a winning spirit about them.

Additionally, a team member must also say yes to the right things on a regular basis. That is, they must say yes to a similar set of morals and integrity the team upholds. They must say yes to being a leader and the leadership styles that the team has in place. They also must say yes to the process and to change. This shows you that a team member has bought into the vision.

The T.H.E.Y. philosophy must also be withheld by you. You have to practice what you preach. Authenticity and culture are a huge part of why great talent chooses to stick with a team.

Another excellent way to build a strong team is by mastering momentum. Momentum is the fuel you receive after you see the progression. No matter how small a step you take in the right direction, it can still serve as motivation for your team to keep going.

I believe that there are two important types of people that you want to be careful to watch; they are momentum breakers and momentum takers. Be very careful of people who do things deliberately to stunt momentum and to hold up the team. Watch equally as close for momentum takers who try and deplete others of their momentum. This could be as simple as someone always talking negative or being pessimistic.

These two attitudes should be addressed swiftly. You must get to the root of it to determine the true reasoning for this type of behavior. If not, you can find your team's momentum draining. As leaders, you must have a niche for clearly identifying these energy types, or it can be crippling for the growth of the team.

When you have a team, you have to be intentional about paying/rewarding them well! It's a balance. Rewards don't have to be monetary all the time, especially if we aren't talking about a business. Sometimes, recognition or speaking a person's love language can be the biggest payment you could ever give to someone.

This is where your emotional intelligence comes into play. Also, where your selflessness can shine. Having a well-cared for team, could be all the difference for them wanting to stay part of the team even when other opportunities exist. Please don't hesitate to let team members know that they are appreciated.

The key takeaway here is to remember to invest in your team as often and as much as you can. Be cognitive of the momentum you and your team have. Build a team to be one of your top assets and build yourself up to be one of the team's top assets.

You also want to operate your life like "Your Name," Inc. You are business all by yourself and have many pieces around you to help. Those could very well be the team that helps you reach levels you couldn't if all alone. Sometimes, we neglect the fact that our lives are connected with a core group of people every day. So be the CEO of your life and build that A1 team you need to thrive. Also, reciprocate the same energy for someone else in your life.

"Teamwork makes the dream work, but a vision becomes a nightmare when the leader has a big dream and a bad team," John C. Maxwell.

This is so true! It's not just enough to have a great dream or vision. You have to have the right team with you to buy into the vision and to execute the plan!

SIXTEEN

RUNNING A PRO-SYSTEM

Study the moves of the highest level in your industry and scale it to your level.

I remember in high school; I joined a CrossFit gym looking for a new way to condition during my offseason from organized sports. I remember in one of my first few classes, our coach explained to us that we all do the same exercises; the only thing that may differ is we may have modifiers.

The philosophy was that even if you couldn't perform the exercise without any modifiers at the moment, you should still be learning the movements and mechanics until you could. We all did the same workouts no matter if we were a beginner or an elite athlete, as long as we physically could.

This idea stuck with me closely and changed the way I viewed life. Besides, there might be a lot of times where we see a certain level we aren't at and think we shouldn't even attempt to follow that regiment. However, we never give ourselves time to learn the degree of scales. Just like in my CrossFit class, our coach knew that there were degrees we could graduate from to reach the highest, so can you in all areas of your life.

So, in life, I challenge you to study the best and the biggest. Learn their operation or "Playbook." Now incorporate those moves into your operations but at a scaled version comparable to your current degree.

Full disclosure, this chapter will use a sports reference to explain. Please bear with me even if you aren't a sports fan at all. This principle can still apply to you also.

First, if you want to play in the same league with the best and the biggest, then you must start running the same operation now, not later. Don't wait to operate at that level until if/when you make it to that level. Operate a modified or scaled-down version of the biggest and the best early.

Time is on your side if you execute this earlier instead of later. You are decreasing your learning curve by being proactive. Remember, you don't become a pro overnight. Also, equally important, you don't become a pro without emulating and practicing LIKE a pro either.

The second concept to keep in mind is you may never know when an opportunity may strike for you to move up. So, you want to practice above the level you currently are in. I even argue to practice the same operations that the absolute elite do. The keyword is PRACTICE. That's because if you mess up in practice, then you can sit down, evaluate it, and try it over and over until you get it right. So, if you have time to work on it until you get it right, then mess up as much as you need until you get it. That way when your opportunity comes, you will recognize it and execute it because you have run your reps.

Think about a professional athlete who started playing their sport in little league. Let's just say that ever since little league, their coach implemented a modified pro-level operation. Of course, this modification was based on the team's age and physical abilities.

The key is the system was built in a way that taught the athlete the game with the end goal in mind. So, as they moved up to high school and college, the system progressively got scaled up to represent even more of the pro-level.

However, something great happened for this future professional; when they leveled up, so did the personnel. Only the ones who adapted and elevated made it to the next level. The number of players also decreased significantly as the level increased. To the point where the odds of becoming a pro were next to nothing.

That's why early is better because you will eternalize so many lessons, the longer you practice it. Of course, when it comes to sport, there are a certain number of teams and spots on a team, so not everyone can make it to play at the highest level.

However, this is life, and I choose to think with an abundance mindset. We all can define a successful life and also what success looks like in business or our profession. Study the moves of the ones you are encouraged by their degree of success.

Study the greats of all backgrounds and learn how to operate at the highest degree. Even if you are trying to do something that was never done before, you still want to study success as a whole.

The key takeaway is you want to run the pro-system early, so that you can internalize it and minimize your learning curve and the barrier to entry for the highest levels. Remember, if you run the pro-system even in the beginning as you mature out of your level, your personnel will grow with you, and you can further execute the "playbook" without having to scale down.

Run a pro-system now! Even while working in the space you're in, you aren't there. You don't want to be called up to the pros and be completely shell shocked. So, it's best to practice and play like a pro no matter what level you're in now. Also, you will always have to work no matter what level you're at because you have to maintain your position at best.

SEVENTEEN

ECO-SYSTEMS OVER PYRAMIDS

"Ecosystem: any system or network of interconnecting and interacting parts, as in a business."

Dictonary.com

It seems like in any business, there is always a hierarchy that leads to a top and a big base. This typically is represented in a pyramid structure. I've always set up by companies to represent spheres.

Pyramids may be the strongest structural shape, but for a successful organization, I believe it's best to build a sphere rather than a pyramid.

Please take a look at the characteristics of a sphere. These three characteristics also help you to see why building a sphere is more beneficial than building a pyramid.

The first characteristic is a perfectly round sphere.

The round shape of a sphere is important because it represents how ecosystems are often represented. In a company, I also felt more comfortable when it was run as an ecosystem vs. a hierarchy. There is more of a sense of belonging and interdependency.

Now, of course, this isn't often the case in many companies, and you are left fighting on the corporate ladder to reach the tip if you choose to. You may always feel easily replaceable or inferior. But in a sphere, you can't find a tip because it is perfectly round.

This is why I've gone as far as making all of my company logos in a circular form. I wanted it to represent inclusion and ecosystem over the corporate ladder and hierarchy.

The second characteristic is spheres are three dimensional.

Being multi-dimensional is important in today's world. You really can't afford to move two dimensional either anymore. I like to look at every deal or "transaction" as three dimensional.

This is because, in the age of the internet and globalization, everything is almost related at any given time. You almost have to account for things to impact at least 3 parties at any given time.

As an example, let's take a real estate deal where on the surface, it appears to be only two parties, the buyer and the seller. Well on many of the biggest deals or even the smallest deals, there is typically at least one more party on the deal. For example, a broker, agent, closing attorney, or an appraiser.

The third characteristic is a sphere that is perfectly symmetrical around its center.

So, it can be argued that the reason why a sphere is the best representation of success to me is because it's perfectly symmetrical around its center. This represents pure harmony because it's hard and maybe even impossible to look at a perfect sphere and find a tip. Now spheres may not have a tip, but they have a center and that is your WHY. It drives everything else in place.

In this same way, I want my company to strive to be like a sphere where it's an ecosystem that promotes harmony and interdependence.

Every point on a sphere is working with each other to create a harmonious sphere. Even though on the surface, you see one shape with its many individual points, it is creating one three dimensional shape.

Now, it may or may not be very apparent how the three used characteristics relate to corporate structure. Nevertheless, with a closer look, I am sure you can see how spheres are more related to the corporate structure of today.

Spheres promote ecosystems, which is how I want to run my company, my life, and how I want to interact with the world.

Study.com defines Sphere as "A geometrical figure that is perfectly round, 3-dimensional and circular - like a ball." I argue that by striving to be a sphere in all that you do, you are promoting an ecosystem by default. Ecosystems, of course, are how we interact with one another and nature, each and every day. That has withstood the test of millions of years.

**FUNDAMENTAL
FOUR**

EIGHTEEN

BLIND FAITH: GOD IS IN
COMPLETE CONTROL

2 Corinthians 5:7 New International Version (NIV) "For we live by faith, not by sight."

Faith is a huge part of my drive. I choose to believe in a God that is bigger than me. Also, I acknowledge that blind faith allows me to relinquish control to God and to believe in the impossible and to accomplish the impossible.

The things I have accomplished thus far are all blessings from the lord. My only true job was to have faith! Faith is something that you do over and over again. You have to practice faith each and every single day.

There is one story I heard growing up that illustrated what exactly faith is. In short, the tightrope walker was able to go back and forth across a serious drop in front of a crowd.

He crossed in very daring ways, including "in a sack, once on stilts, another time on a bicycle, and once he even carried a stove and cooked an omelet!" www.CreativeBiblestudy.com says. He then crossed blindfolded with a wheelbarrow. The story then continues to say

"'Do you believe I can carry a person across in this wheelbarrow?' Of course, the crowd shouted that yes, they believed! It was then that Blondin posed the question - 'Who will get in the wheelbarrow?' Of course...none did."

The moral of the story is that it is easy to say you have blind faith, but really it is blind faith that is taking action. If the crowd really had faith, then they would have gotten in the wheelbarrow.

The wild thing is, the crowd saw with their very own eyes the feat done. In life, we don't always get to preview what we are about to put our faith into. God wants us to live by faith and not by sight.

So, when we say we have faith, it's like saying we will get in the wheelbarrow to cross the tightrope but without the luxury of seeing the tightrope cross successfully. That's not easy to do by any means. It's a conscious choice. However, when you believe in a loving and gracious God, you are OK with relinquishing control to let God move.

The key takeaway here is that you have to faith it to make it! Not fake it to make it! Faking it is saying you have faith, but when it comes to putting actions behind it, you don't move.

Besides, faith is also an action that we take intentionally. It's moving even if you don't see what is beyond the next step. That's trust and the more I learn this every day, the less pressure I feel. God will show you just how loving he is and how gracious he is when you have faith.

It starts with very small gestures of faith, like believing what the bible says and having faith that God loves you. Faith can also grow huge into believing in the huge loving promises God has for each and every one of us.

NINETEEN

ETHICS

Matthew 7:12 New Living Translation (NLT) The Golden Rule 12 "Do to others whatever you would like them to do to you. This is the essence of all that is taught in the law and the prophets."

Integrity is your legacy. You may say it's nothing personal, it's just business; but it is in your decisions, in how you choose to treat those who can do nothing for you, that tells a lot about who you are.

You can have had massive success and still have ethics. Sometimes people buy into the misconception that very successful people are corrupt and have no morals. There are bad players at all degrees of life. Withholding high ethics is a choice one makes.

As you find yourself succeeding more and more, you may see opportunities to go against your morals to cut corners. This is a trap! It's never worth the "shortcut" to reach a goal.

Never forget your integrity! This is non-negotiable. Being honest will keep your name clean and open many more doors than dishonesty will. The more you succeed, the more your integrity will be challenged. Success doesn't give you a pass to do whatever you want. It creates more responsibility for you to do the right thing.

Integrity is doing the right thing when no one is looking. You have to discipline yourself to do the right thing, no matter what. It's not just about looking good when people can see what you do. You have to ask yourself; would I do the right thing even if no one is there to pin flowers on me?

That is how we all can change the world to be a better place, even if just a little bit. Keeping ethics in our lives, our businesses, politics, relationships, and on and on. Following this simple gesture will spark a domino effect around you, causing others to join in.

This is extremely crucial when you are also a leader because you set the tone for those who trust you as a leader. The message you set trickles down to all those around you. You choosing to dishonor your ethics can not only hurt your team but also influence them to take on the same attitude.

In life, there is nothing worth compromising your integrity over. It's not only your reputation on the line but also, people's trust in you could be destroyed. Trust is earned, and it's not easy to earn back. Be very careful thinking that you can buy your way back in good books with those after you get what you want.

The same is true about those around you. Be very mindful of how people withhold their integrity. Read people's actions versus their words; are they congruent, or is there a disconnect?

There's a wise saying that goes something like, when people show you who they are, believe them the first time around. This is pretty spot on. People sometimes put on a mask to make a good first impression. They want to look the best and cover any imperfections. This is pretty normal and nothing too alarming. However, as people get more comfortable, they tend to let down the mask and show you more of them. If they do this, it will be a great opportunity to see who they are.

In those moments, you have to believe what you see. If it's there, it must be addressed if the situation allows for it. As a leader, it can be a great coaching moment. If the other person is willing to address the moment where they slipped judgment and went against their ethics, only then can you be in a position where you can help them out. I urge you to do so as well as helping to encourage them to withhold their ethics.

One hard duty of a leader is also to recognize when a person isn't willing to grow. If they are willing to compromise their ethics and don't intend to change, it might be best to separate yourself from that energy. This mindset will hinder your growth and the growth of your team. The last thing you want is for this to potentially become normalized.

TWENTY

GIVE IT ALL AWAY

Proverbs 11:25 New International Version (NIV) 25 "A generous person will prosper; whoever refreshes others will be refreshed."

There's no better feeling than to be able to help others and not to look for anything in return. To help educate, motivate, empower is like no other. That's what it's all about for me when I look at my core values.

The "Give it all away" concept came to me from a co-worker of mine at a grocery store I worked at right after college. When I first heard it, I was bewildered why anyone would do such a thing. That's because I had a scarcity mindset. Now I know that's a call to action like no other.

Giving it all away is a dare to believe in abundance rather than scarcity. When you believe there's not enough in the world, then you wouldn't fathom giving it all away. What I came to realize that the truth is the more you give, the more it comes back to you. This is true with money and even more so with serving others.

Mark 10:29-31 MSG says Jesus said, "Mark my words, no one who sacrifices house, brothers, sisters, mother, father, children, land—whatever—because of me and the Message will lose out. They'll get it all back, but multiplied many times in homes, brothers, sisters, mothers, children, and land—but also in troubles. And then the bonus of eternal life! This is once again the Great Reversal: Many who are first will end up last, and the last first."

The last part, to me, speaks on serving others. A leader may lead to a position that puts them in front, but in all actuality, a true leader is a servant. To serve others, you can't put yourself first. You make sacrifices for the betterment of those you serve.

This is giving it all away to me. It's not meant to make sense because it's not normal. It takes faith to do what's not normal and give your all to serve others.

Once you do it and see the wonderful impact you make, you will look around and see you can never out give. Things have a funny way of coming back to you multiplied when you lock in and serve others for their benefit.

It will feel better than anything you can splurge your time and money on. It's not a crime to want to do and have nice things. It's simply a matter of prioritizing. The more blessed you are, the more of a blessing you can be.

One key thing is also that you don't have to wait to serve; you can start from wherever you are. Serve where you can and just be careful not to neglect your necessities and functions. You can still live a thriving life and give it all away.

For me, there are three levels I always strive to serve in. Those are Family and Friends, Community, and Globally.

Family and friends could very well be the closest to you. Odds are if you have good relations with your family and friends, this may be the most frequent area you will serve in.

I look to serve my family and friends because I know I wouldn't be where I am if it wasn't for them. Their support, love, and encouragement helped me push through the downs and kept me humble during the victories.

Serving at this level lets your loved ones know you care about them and you appreciate all that they do for you. It also shows them that they are important to you, and you care to see them have a great quality of life also.

The next level is the community. This is what I like to say is your local or national community. There are many causes and groups that we can support here in our borders. Even in our very own neighborhoods and cities, there are many ways to serve others.

My father always told me never to forget where you come from. I lived in a few cities growing up and make it my mission not to forget the people there.

Also, you can look into a cause that goes nationwide. Many causes are not only happening in your neighborhood but also in other neighborhoods too. I look for opportunities to help in places that I am also not physically as well.

This leads us to our last level, which is Global. The world is bigger than just one neighborhood, one nation, one continent. There are causes that we can support globally. There are even causes that impact everyone and everything on the globe. Looking to serve in opportunities that benefit others globally, which is equally as important.

The key takeaway here is the love of money is the root of all evil. Money is just a tool and makes you more of who you already are. On the flip side, if you see money as the vehicle to be extremely generous, you can see a ton of good come from wealth.

Like my pastor says, giving is more than money but also about the quality of life. You don't have to be rich at all to serve others. You can help someone reach a better quality of life in many ways other than things or money. Take, for example, serving others with your time or even sharing your knowledge. The list can go on and on.

Money is an area where people who strive for success forget to serve others with. That tight grip you may have on your money can hinder you from reaching true fulfillment. It's not bad to have ambitions to build wealth. The key is to remember that with more, you have the opportunity to give it all away. You can give like no one else.

Dave Ramsey said best "The peace in financial peace comes from being outrageous generosity" and also "God owns it all. We are just asset managers for the Lord."

CONCLUSION

You have made it through all four sections of this book; focus, finances, faculty, and faith. There is no secret to success. You will hear a lot on your journey. This book is no different.

What this book and other books like it do, is serve as a reminder that it's possible. We all have our own paths and our own purpose in life, when we get to read other perspectives from those who are striving to help better you, to learn through others.

The biggest teacher is experiencing, but you can also learn how to navigate the roads better through others. That's why there's no room for the ego because it will blur your ability to be receptive.

Whatever you pursue in life, I want you to know that you don't have to lose yourself in the journey. You matter just the way you are on any given day because you are here. Don't ever let anyone or anything make you feel any less than the next. Life is an incredible gift, and any new day you get, you can make the most of it.

Success isn't meant to change you for the worst. Those are traps. Also, who's to say what success has to look like. Living a fulfilled life is your story to write.

As an author, my only goal was to inspire and share steps you can take. I wanted you to see that the sky isn't the limit, but there's much much more. I wanted to help demystify the notion that there is an "elite" space you can't reach. Who's to say you're not destined to enter this so-called "elite" space and create positive change.

Love can and will prevail over hatred. Love doesn't make you weak but strong. Master your emotions, and don't let them master you.

I enjoy building up others. It thrills me to see others grow and succeed. It all goes back to having an abundance mindset. I have no time for a scarcity mindset. I hope that in reading this book, I have added some value to your journey.

I believe that you can and will succeed. I am confident because I know that you will start by mastering your mindset. You proved it by investing in learning.

I believe in your success, what about you?

ABOUT
THE
AUTHOR

Kerry Hartley, a serial entrepreneur, is CEO of Hartley Capital Inc. He is an author, speaker, coach, and volunteer. He has always had an interest in entrepreneurship from an early age. After graduating from Florida Agricultural and Mechanical University (FAMU), he pursued his dreams of launching his own company. Visit his website at www.KerryLeeHartley.com